University of Virginia
The Lawn

Phaidon Press Ltd
140 Kensington Church Street
London W8 4BN

First published 1994

ISBN 0 7148 2752 5

A CIP catalogue record for this book is available
from the British Library

Printed in Singapore

University of Virginia
The Lawn
Thomas Jefferson

Michael Brawne
ARCHITECTURE IN DETAIL

Φ

4

1 Henri Isaac Browere: Thomas Jefferson, 1825. This cast was made from a life mask the year before Jefferson's death and during a period when he was still working on the University of Virginia as an architect and also as Rector of the Board of Visitors.
2 Thomas Jefferson: study for changes to the Hôtel de Langeac, Paris, 1785. Jefferson lived here during most of his stay in Paris as minister to France from 1784 to 1789. He also proposed changes for the extensive wedge-shaped garden of the house.
3 The Rotunda, Pavilions II, IV and the corner of VI at the University of Virginia.

1

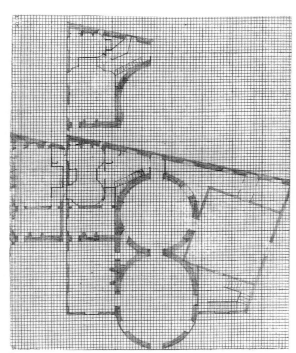

2

The architect

Thomas Jefferson was meticulous about life, architecture and death. Among the thousands of letters, notes and drawings that have been preserved, there is a page on which Jefferson leaves instructions about his tombstone and the inscription it was to carry. There was to be 'on the grave a plain die or cube of 3f. without any mouldings, surmounted by an obelisk of 6f. height, each of a single stone'. The inscription was to read:

Here was buried
Thomas Jefferson
Author of the Declaration of
American Independence
of the Statute of Virginia for religious freedom
& Father of the University of Virginia.

In his note he added below this: 'because by these, as testimonials that I have lived, I wish most to be remembered'. Equally significantly, perhaps, the specification for the words was preceded by the injunction, 'the following inscription and not one word more'.[1]

Yet Jefferson had in the eighty-three years of his life (1743–1826) been noted for many considerable achievements. He had been a man at the centre of the political and intellectual life of the newly independent United States. More than anyone else, he was the philosopher statesman of the new republic. Jefferson studied law and was admitted to the Bar; became an elected burgess to the Virginia Assembly; was elected to the Continental Congress in Philadelphia; then elected Governor of Virginia. He was appointed to succeed Benjamin Franklin as minister to France where he spent four years in Paris. On his return he became Secretary of State during George Washington's presidency. He was elected Vice President of the United States in 1796 and President in 1801. During his first term he concluded the purchase of Louisiana from France; he was re-elected for a second term in 1804. Throughout this period he was also deeply concerned about agriculture, natural history, music, friendship and his family, and the philosophical and moral questions with which his contemporaries grappled. Principal among these were the notions of equality, freedom and slavery, the nature of education, and the intentions underlying the Creation and how these affect our actions.

But most significantly, Jefferson was, throughout his life, always a builder in the sense that he concerned himself with the everyday activities of the site; he calculated the number of bricks required for a building, ordered material and organized labour. Most of this activity was concentrated on his home in Monticello on the crown of a hill above Charlottesville in the foothills of Virginia. He started work at Monticello in 1768 when he was twenty-five and more or less concluded it over forty years later when he retired there at the end of his second term as President in 1809. Wherever he spent any length of time he had an apparently irresistible desire to alter buildings; he did so at the Governor's Palace at Williamsburg and at his residence in Paris, the Hôtel de Langeac, where he also redesigned the garden. His drive to mould the environment was a deep passion and it is this which made him an architect for most of his life.

Jefferson saw architecture as an expression of people's ideas and aspirations and it mattered to him enormously that the buildings of the new republic should be based on the best available models since the new nation had no models of its own. The past was to be the starting point for a new and different future. First and dominant among these sources was Andrea Palladio. Jefferson owned a copy of Giacomo Leoni's translation *The Architecture of A. Palladio; in four books*, which was published in 1715. The first architectural books which it is thought Jefferson bought while still a student at William and Mary College in Williamsburg were *A Book of Architecture* by James Gibbs and Palladio's *Quatro Libri*.[2] Although Jefferson was later to be greatly influenced by French neo-classical architecture, Palladio remained the fountainhead and touchstone. That Palladio's architecture flourished in a cultured agrarian community – akin to Jefferson's own ambitions for Virginia and the new United States – undoubtedly reinforced its relevance.

An intellectual group existed around Padua and Vicenza in the middle of the 16th century, many of whom were Palladio's patrons. Jefferson also belonged to such a group and was probably its most influential member. Others include Benjamin Franklin, thirty-seven years older than Jefferson; David Rittenhouse, the astronomer, engineer and first director of the United States Mint; Benjamin Rush, doctor of medicine, professor of chemistry, signatory of the Declaration of Independence; Joseph Priestley, the discoverer of oxygen; Thomas Paine, author of the *Rights of Man* and *The Age of Reason* and several others who came to be called the Jeffersonian Circle.[3]

The establishment of a new university away from the population centres of the East Coast conformed exactly to these ideals. Jefferson concerned himself equally with the political manoeuvres that were necessary to ensure its successful birth as with its architecture. It is the crowning achievement of his old age.

4

5

Earlier projects

Jefferson had no professional architectural education. He consulted a wide range of architectural books and was always keen to observe and comment. The architecture that he most admired could be described by certain rules and precepts. These were largely to be found in books. Jefferson went on a brief visit to Italy in 1787 mainly to study the possible application of methods of rice growing in the Po valley to agriculture in the Southern States. He never saw a building by Palladio. He did, however, spend time observing and admiring the new buildings of Paris during his stay there between 1785 and 1789. He was, as he wrote, 'violently smitten'[4] by the Hôtel de Salm, which was then under construction and which was to affect the second version of Monticello on his return to the latter in December 1793. Neo-classicism was later to exert a significant influence on the University of Virginia.

Most of the plans that Jefferson drew were done on graph paper. This was divided into 1 inch squares, which in turn were divided into ten parts. The usual scale was thus $\frac{1}{10}$ inch equals 1 foot. The co-ordinate lines were sometimes grey, occasionally red. He drew in both ink and pencil. The reverse side of the drawing frequently contained a specification. Many sketch plans show calculations in the margin and demonstrate the mathematical sequence used to derive dimensions. Since so many of these depend on ratios, the end result is often given to three decimal places. There is no record of how his workmen coped with such precision.

Monticello is the building that is most readily associated with Jefferson. This is partly due to the fact that he devoted such a large proportion of his life to its construction, that it was the place where he thought himself most content and that it is now open to the public. Very large numbers of people still come to pay homage and to satisfy their curiosity about a man still very much in the American consciousness.

Architecturally, Monticello is not of the first rank. Vincent Scully has gone so far as to say 'Compared to the Villa Rotonda, majestic on the hill, Burlington's Chiswick is an impertinence and Jefferson's Monticello looks positively tacky'.[5] The judgement may be harsh and can certainly not be applied to

many other projects by Jefferson, least of all to the University of Virginia.

What is masterly at Monticello is Jefferson's disposition of elements on the ground. He uses the Palladian plan form of a central pavilion with lower extensions to the left and right, but makes these extensions into raised boarded terraces below which, buried in the ground, are the kitchen, dairy, smoke house, ice house, wine cellar and other service rooms, and the stables and carriage bays. The service area is thus linked under cover and communicates directly with the house but is entirely unobtrusive. This disposition was made possible by putting the building on the crown of the hill while at the same time allowing the panoramic view from the house to be exploited clear of any obstruction.

The gardens were also laid out by Jefferson who had a great interest in botany and landscape. For instance, he kept meticulous records about the times he planted his vegetable seeds and when the produce was ready for the table. In 1786 when he went to England with John Adams (who preceded him as president) the gardens of country houses were the main objective of the visit. He wrote to his friend John Page: 'The gardening in that country is the article in which it surpasses all the earth. I mean their pleasure gardening. This, indeed, went far beyond my ideas'.[6] The English landscape tradition was to remain his enthusiasm rather than the French, despite the unfavourable political overtones that anything English often had for Jefferson.

In 1780 Jefferson was appointed head of a committee that was to oversee the

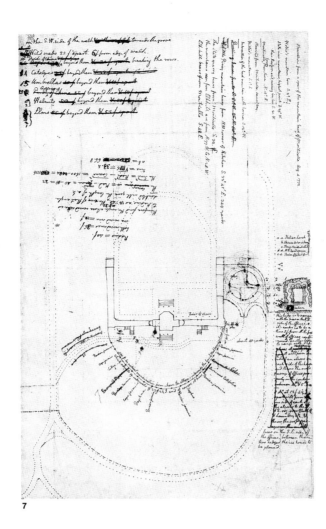

7

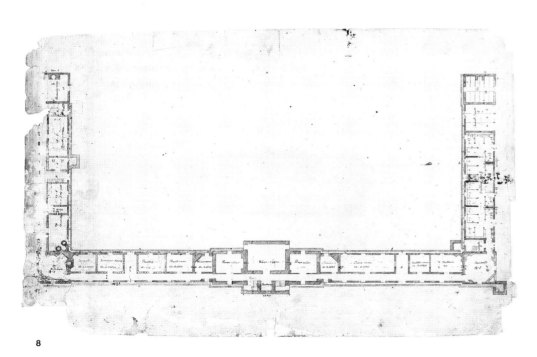

8

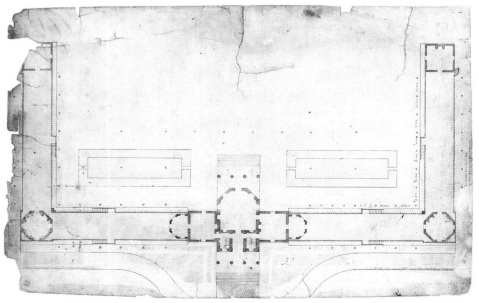

9

4 The construction of the Hôtel de Salm (signed Faldot, Jaldot or Jallot), 1784. Jefferson was greatly attracted by this building; he watched the construction almost daily while in Paris. It had a considerable influence on the revised design for Monticello.

5 Andrea Palladio: Villa Almerico or Rotonda, begun 1565/66.

6 Lord Burlington: Chiswick Villa, London, begun c.1725.

7 Thomas Jefferson: general plan of the summit of Monticello mountain, after 2 August 1771 and before 4 August 1772. The drawing shows the final plan, including the dependencies; the names of trees and shrubs are given. Jefferson also notes a trigonometrical calculation for setting out.

8 Thomas Jefferson: final drawing of the basement and dependencies of Monticello, before August 1772. Because of the slope of the ground the dependencies are below the garden level of the house, though the left- and right-hand sides have an outlook where the ground slopes away steeply.

9 Thomas Jefferson: final drawing of the ground floor of Monticello with dependencies, 1772–84. The drawing was frequently altered up until the time of Jefferson's departure for Paris in 1784. The roof of the dependencies is a terrace of wooden boards with a waterproof roof below. The octagonal pavilions in the corners were never built.

erection of public buildings in Richmond, the new state capital of Virginia. In that year, or very soon after, Jefferson produced a number of drawings for the Governor's House. He also prepared drawings for the Virginia Capitol, which was to be a simple temple-form structure with a portico at each end. The design was discussed with Charles-Louis Clerisseau during Jefferson's stay in France and it was probably he who suggested the omission of one portico and the change from Corinthian to Ionic. A model was made in France and sent to Richmond at the end of 1786. The resemblance to the Maison Carrée in Nîmes is close and was acknowledged by Jefferson. He once wrote to his friend Mme de Tessé: 'Here I am, Madam, gazing whole hours at the Maison Quarrée like a lover at his mistress'. During construction the design unfortunately was simplified further and changes were made in material in order to reduce the cost of the scheme.

Jefferson's involvement with the Capitol as well as the Penitentiary, although he was absent from France, shows the interest he took in Virginia and his deep desire to steer the course of architecture in his state along the lines that he thought most appropriate. This was not the dabbling of an amateur but the involvement of someone concerned with the rehabilitation of criminals, the nature of spaces for the government of the new republic and the relation of such questions to architecture.

For similarly complex reasons Jefferson involved himself with the creation of the new federal capital in Washington and with two of its most important public buildings, the President's House (later to be called the White House) and the Capitol, in which the House of Representatives and the Senate were to have their chambers. He was able to do so as Secretary of State during Washington's presidency, especially as Washington had no particular interest in architecture. One of the most important issues was how to achieve, in the impecunious new state, a measure of grandeur that also demonstrated the required degree of republican simplicity.

It was due to Jefferson's political manoeuvres that the capital of the United States was sited on the banks of the Potomac rather than the Hudson or Delaware rivers. In 1791 he sketched out a grid-iron plan for the city. At that time he argued in a note above the plan: 'Will it not be best to lay out the long streets parallel with the Creek, and the other crossing them at right angles, so as to leave no oblique angled lots but the single row which shall be on the river'.[7]

Pierre-Charles L'Enfant who had come over from France to fight in the American War of Independence as an engineer, and who later converted New York's city hall where Congress met and Washington was inaugurated, was called in to survey the site and to lay out plans for the federal city. He was to report progress twice a week by letter to Jefferson. Perhaps because he was delayed by weather, L'Enfant wrote asking for plans of important European cities. Jefferson was able to respond immediately: 'I have exam-ined my papers and found plans of Frankfort on the Mayne, Carlsruhe, Amsterdam, Strasburg, Paris, Orleans, Bordeaux, Lyon, Montpellier, Marseilles, Turin and Milan, which I send in a roll by this Post. They are on large and accurate scales, having been procured by me while in these respective cities myself'.[8]

As it turned out, L'Enfant did not model his design on any of these cities but very closely on Le Nôtre's plan for Versailles of 1670. In 1792 L'Enfant quarrelled with the commissioners of the federal city, was dismissed and much of the execution was left to Jefferson.

The position of the two main public buildings was now established in the plan; the Capitol corresponded to the palace at Versailles, the president's house to the Grand Trianon. Jefferson therefore was able to turn his attention to the design and construction of these key monuments. He proposed a competition and drafted the advertisement, which was issued by the city commissioners. Although he was Secretary of State at the time, Jefferson submitted an entry anonymously, which was very much based on Palladio's Villa Rotonda. He was not present at the judging – probably deliberately – and the entry by James Hoban, an Irish-born professional architect, was selected.

Similarly, a competition was held for the design of the Capitol, which was won by an amateur architect, Dr William Thornton. Jefferson sketched designs for the Capitol based on a rotunda. The plan was divided into four oval rooms around a central space with a stair, very much

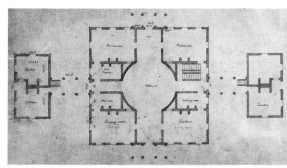

10

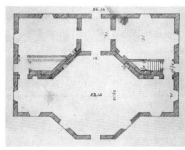

11

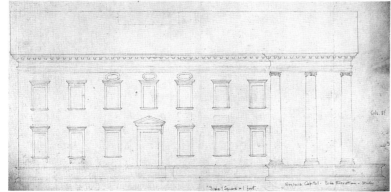

12

13

14

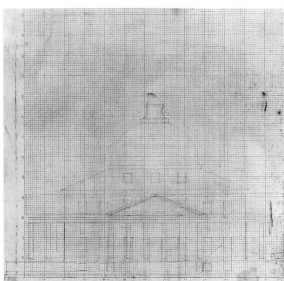

15

10 Thomas Jefferson: ground floor plan of the Governor's House, Richmond, c.1780. This design features an octagonal room, a device which is also seen in Jefferson's plans for Monticello and Poplar Forest.

11 Thomas Jefferson: study for the Governor's House, Richmond, Virginia, 1780.

12 Thomas Jefferson: side elevation of the Virginia Capitol. The design was revised after Jefferson arrived in France in 1794

13 Maison Carrée, Nîmes, probably 16 BC. The best-preserved Roman temple in existence, which Jefferson greatly admired.

14 Thomas Jefferson: west front of Monticello, 1769–1809.

15, 16 Thomas Jefferson: the President's House, Washington. Preliminary study for the competition design, 1792. This design, based on Palladio's Villa Rotonda, was submitted anonymously by Jefferson. The entry may have been prompted by Jefferson's concern that the President's House should go beyond the accepted level of provincial architecture.

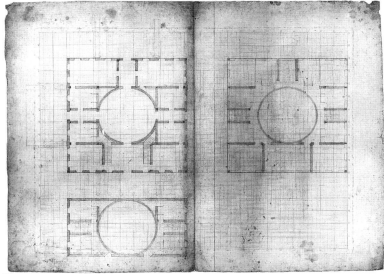

16

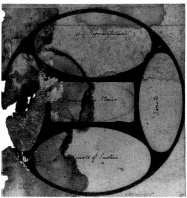

17

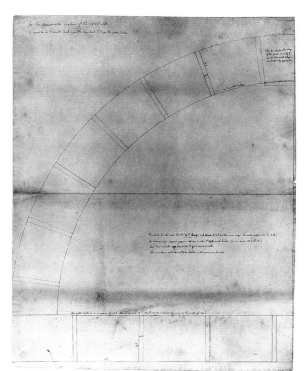

18

19

like John-Nicolas Le Rouge's Désert de Retz Column House, which Jefferson had seen while in Paris. He was to use the same theme when planning the Rotunda at the University of Virginia.

There were considerable difficulties with Thornton's plan for the Capitol and the supervision of its construction. Eventually in 1803, Jefferson, who was by then President, appointed Benjamin Latrobe as surveyor of the public buildings. Jefferson, however, continued to interfere; he made suggestions about the ceiling of the House of Representatives and requested details of the drainage of skylights, since he wanted to ensure that the chamber would be suffused with light like the Halle aux Bled, the grain market he had admired in Paris. Whatever the project, he always had a precedent in mind.

The University of Virginia

In 1809 Jefferson completed his second term as President and retired to his house in Monticello above Charlottesville, making occasional visits to his retreat, Poplar Forest, a wonderfully pure octagonal house he had designed for himself on the estate left to him by his wife. By that time he had not only held the highest offices of state but had also been involved with the design of a number of houses and public buildings. He knew about construction and the problems of the site. He had become, through experience, a professional architect even though he often turned to other architects for advice or suggestions. He could by then properly be described as the first great native-born architect of the United States, although his masterwork was still to come.

The idea of a new university in Virginia and thoughts about the planning of an educational institution had been with Jefferson long before the founding of a college was considered officially. As early as 1800 he wrote to his friend Dr Joseph Priestley: 'We wish to establish in the upper country, and more centrally for the State, a University on a plan so broad and liberal and modern, as to be worth patronizing with the public support, and be a temptation to the youth of other states to come to drink the cup of knowledge and fraternize with us'.[9]

Ten years later, and seven years before he was asked to prepare plans, forms were already being defined, at least verbally, which are very close to the final outcome: 'The common plan followed in this country of making one large expensive building, I consider as unfortunately erroneous. It is infinitely better to erect a small separate lodge for each separate professorship, with only a hall below for his class, and two chambers above for himself; joining these lodges by barracks for a certain portion of the students, opening into a covered way, to give dry communication between all of the schools. The whole of these arranged around an open square of grass and trees, would make it, what it should be in fact, an academical village'.[10]

Two aspects are significant: the notion of a teacher as an individual who lived among a group of students making both a social and an educational community and the placement of that community in a landscape setting as if it were a village. That this community would consist of free men was not an issue under debate; neither women nor slaves had a place at a university.

As in the case of the siting of the city of Washington, the first hurdles were political and concerned themselves again with the rival claims of different locations. Jefferson had encouraged a friend, Joseph Carrington Cabell, to enter the House of Delegates of the State of Virginia and from there he transferred to the Senate. With Cabell's support, the State legislature passed an act in February 1816 which founded an institution to be called Central College in Charlottesville. Equally crucially Thomas Jefferson was to be one of the seven visitors charged with overseeing the establishment of the college. Eventually he and only one other visitor, General John Hartwell Cocke, were to be in charge of planning and financial matters.

As soon as the site and Jefferson's suggestions were approved on 5 May 1817, Jefferson put his ideas on paper; on 9 May he wrote to Dr Thornton, the winner of the Washington Capitol competition, and to Latrobe on 12 June giving each a sketch of a possible layout and asking for advice. The description of his proposal went into considerable detail and, although significant developments were to occur, the essential elements are outlined in the sketch and description:

20

21

22

23

24

17 Thomas Jefferson: study for the Capitol building, Washington, 1792.

18 Thomas Jefferson (probably drawn by his daughter Cornelia Jefferson Randolph: ground floor plan, c.1820, of Poplar Forest, south of Lychburg. Jefferson designed this retreat for himself on the 4300-acre estate bequeathed to him by his wife; it is his purest development of the octagonal plan.

19 Thomas Jefferson: semi-circular window detail of Monticello, c.1803. This is a full-size detail. Jefferson notes that 'the arch bricks are to be 9.1 long, 3.1 thick, and 3.1 on the inner edge. The outer edge will be 3‰.'

20 The double staircase, which rises through two floors of the Rotunda, is the first double stair in North America. The central doors relate the inner space to the long axis of the Lawn.

21 The library on the top floor of the Rotunda is the largest interior space in Jefferson's design for the university. It was clearly based on the Pantheon in Rome; unlike the Pantheon, however, it had two upper level galleries. The ceiling of the dome room was covered with ill-fitting sound-absorbing panels during the restoration work of the 1970s.

22 The pavilions on the west side. Pavilion I on the right is based on the Doric Order taken from Diocletian's Baths in Rome, Pavilion II on the opposite side of the Lawn uses the Ionic order, the Rotunda between them is Corinthian.

23 The colonnade on the west side. The Ionic columns of Pavilion V rise through two floors; the student rooms on the left form the link between individual pavilions.

24 An interior view of the Pantheon in Rome, built in the 2nd century.

We are commencing here the establishment of a college, and instead of building a magnificent house which could exhaust all our funds, we propose to lay off a square of about 7. or 800. f. wide, the outside of which we shall arrange separate pavilions, one for each professor and his scholars. Each pavilion will have a schoolroom below, and 2 rooms for the professor above and between pavilion and pavilion a range of dormitories for the boys, one story high, giving to each room 10f. wide and 12 f. deep. The pavilions about 36 wide in front and 24 f. in depth. this sketch will give you an idea of it. the whole of the pavilions and dormitories to be united by a colonnade in front of the height of the lower story of the pavilions, under which they may go dry from school to school. the colonnade will be of square brick pilasters (at first) with a Tuscan entablature. now what we wish is that these pavilions as will show themselves above the dormitories, shall be models of taste & good architecture, & of a variety of appearance, no two alike, so as to serve as specimens of the Architectural lectures. Will you set your imagination to work & sketch some designs for us, no matter how loosely with the pen, without the trouble of referring to scale or rule; for we want nothing but the outline of the architecture, as the internal must be arranged according to local convenience a few sketches such as need not take you a moment will greatly oblige us…[11]

Latrobe replied on 24 July 1817 by sending a sketch, showing a hierarchically important building as the centre of the composition, '…which ought to exhibit in Mass & details as perfect a specimen of good Architectural taste as can be devised. I should propose *below*, a couple or 4 rooms for Janitors or Tutors, above, a room for Chemical or other lectures, above a circular lecture room under the dome…'.[12] Thornton sent two drawings, one of which was really for a single neo-classical palace with occasional two-storeyed porticos; certainly not an 'academical village'.

During this year Jefferson drew quite a number of precise drawings for individual pavilions on his usual graph paper, particularly for what was eventually to be numbered Pavilion VII. This was the first to be constructed. The ten pavilions are numbered as on a street with even numbers on one side, odd numbers on the other and with numbers I and II opposite each other at the head, nearest the Rotunda. These drawings show very clearly a temple form for the pavilion with student rooms as a single-storey link. The rooms were entered from the continuous covered way, which was surmounted by Chinese lattice railings, similar to those Jefferson had used at Monticello. Each room had a fireplace and the chimneys just protruded above the railings, just as they did above the terrace that covered the sunken service wings at Monticello.

In a sense the open U-shaped form of the university was an enlarged version of Monticello and its two wings. Both of course go back to several of the villas illustrated in the second book of Palladio's *Quatro Libri*, where 'the sta-

bles, the cellars, the granaries, and such like other places, for the use of the villa, are on each side of the court'.[13] Palladio's villas and their outbuildings were as a rule farm complexes, the centre of working estates. This agrarian basis for the disposition of building elements would have appealed to Jefferson who envisioned the new republic as having just such a farming foundation; one suspects that he needed an intellectual argument to underpin his visual preferences. His belief in the importance of agriculture extended to it as a subject of study. In 1803 he wrote that agriculture: 'is the first in utility, and ought to be the first in respect. The same artificial means which have been used to produce a competition in learning, may be equally successful in restoring agriculture to its primary dignity in the eyes of men. It is a science of the very first order… In every College and University, a professorship of agriculture, and the class of its students, might be honored as the first…closing their academical education with this, as the crown of all other sciences…'.[14] Such an emphasis on utility was to colour the curriculum taught at the new University of Virginia.

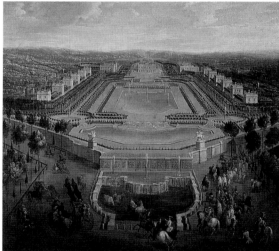

25

26

27

Dear Sir   Monticello May 9.17

Your favor of yr 18 was duly received, and the two draw-
-ings were delivered here by mr & mrs Madison in perfect good order.
with respect to Cerracchi's bust, any artist whom you dispose to
do so shall be welcome to come and make a cast of plaister from it.
we have always plaister at home.

We are commencing here the establishment of a college, and instead
of building a magnificent house which would exhaust all our funds, we propose
to lay off a square of about 7. or 800.   the outside of which we shall
arrange separate pavilions, one for each professor and his scholars.   each
pavilion will have a schoolroom below, and 2 rooms for the Professor above
and   pavilion and pavilion a range of dormitories for the boys, one
story high, giving to each a room 10.f. wide & 14.f. deep. the pavilions
36. wide in front and 24.f. in depth. this sketch will give you an idea of it

grass & trees

the whole of the pavilions and dormitories to be united by a colonnade, in
front of the height of the lower story of the pavilions, under which they may
go dry from school to school. the colonnade will be of square brick pilasters
(at first) with a Tuscan entablature. now what we wish is that these pavilions
as they will shew themselves above the dormitories, shall be models of taste &
good architecture, & of a variety of appearance, no two alike; so as to serve as
specimens for the Architectural lectures. will you set your imagina-
-tion to work & sketch some designs for us. no matter how loosely with

Dr. Thornton

25 Pierre-Denis Martin, le Jeune: Château de Marly (1679), painted in 1724. In 1786 Jefferson visited Marly in the company of Maria Cosway. The layout has been described as 'a colony of gazebos rather than a palace', an idea that may have influenced the University of Virginia.
26 The three-bay temple front of Pavilion IV on the east side. Jefferson's original design drawing is annotated 'Doric of Albano' and has a door in the centre of the elevation.
27 The facade of Pavilion III on the west side has a two-storey portico, which is narrower than the house. The Corinthian capitals are Carrara marble and may be partly the reason why this was the most expensive of all pavilions to construct; it was also originally the largest.
28 Thomas Jefferson: early plan of the University of Virginia, 9 May 1817. Jefferson's preliminary ideas for the university were sketched as part of a letter he wrote to Dr Thornton asking for architectural advice; all the elements that were finally built are present in this outline.

29 Benjamin Latrobe: sketch for the University of Virginia, 24 July 1817. Latrobe replied to Jefferson's request for advice on the project in a letter, which showed an amended layout with an important building at the centre.

30 Thomas Jefferson: study for the plan and elevations of a pavilion and flanking dormitories for Central College, (later Pavilion VII) of the University of Virginia, 1817. This was the first pavilion to be built and is in the middle of the west side. Central College became the University of Virginia in 1819. The ground floor plan shows a large class room entered directly from the continuous covered passage.

31 View down the Lawn from the portico of the Rotunda. The vista is closed by Cabell Hall, which was built at the end of the 19th century, thus losing Jefferson's sense of openness on the downhill side.

32 The north side of the Rotunda by Stanford White. It was erected after the fire of 1895 when the large North Annexe, which had been built in 1851, was not replaced. This side now faces the town and thus becomes the normal approach to the Jefferson precinct.

33 John Wood, the Younger: Royal Crescent, Bath, begun 1767. The design juxtaposes building against open countryside by leaving half the oval open on the downhill side; in this respect it is very similar to the open rectangle at the University of Virginia.

34 Thomas Jefferson (drawing probably shaded by Cornelia Jefferson Randolph): bird's-eye view of the University of Virginia, c.1820. A view from the east showing the two inner rows of pavilions and dormitory link blocks, and the two outer rows of hotels and dormitories. The slopes and garden sub-divisions are omitted; the Rotunda had not yet been built.

14

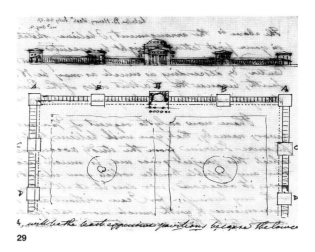

29

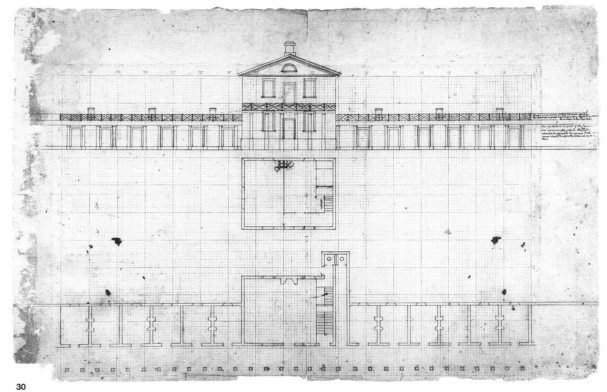

30

31

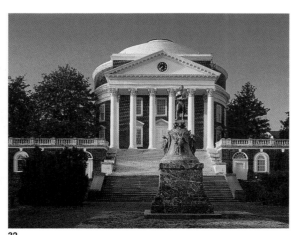

32

Jefferson was also, naturally, influenced by the architecture he saw while in France. He was particularly impressed by neo-classicism and its preference for simple and often dominantly horizontal forms. In 1786 on a visit to the Château de Marly in the Ile-de-France he was greatly impressed by the buildings, the gardens and the elaborate and mechanically-fascinating waterworks. Jules-Hardouin Mansart had designed this complex for Louis XIV in 1679. The plan consisted of a U-shaped garden, at the head of which was the principal building for the Sun King. This was flanked on either side by six pavilions for the courtiers, each pavilion standing for a sign of the zodiac. The buildings were linked by terraces, pergolas and avenues of trees. Marly may have remained especially memorable since Jefferson, then a widower, saw it in the company of Maria Cosway, an artist with whom he was deeply in love.

What is important is that Marly was not only a memory but that it chimed with dominant Palladian ideas and that these had already been successfully put into effect at Monticello. Here, at the university, as in most instances, the most influential sources are the architect's own previous designs.

Marly and Palladio's villas of the Veneto moreover conformed to a neo-classical perception of the juxtaposition of buildings and landscapes of which the design for the Royal Crescent in Bath by John Wood the Younger, started in 1767, is probably the most outstanding planning example. The Crescent is a kind of harbour into which the landscape flows while the buildings look out into the open country. This is quite different from baroque urban enclosure.

In 1817 an old cornfield of 43¾ acres (17.7 hectares) was purchased for the College. Jefferson – then seventy-four years old – surveyed it in the heat of July and started to grade it with a team of ten men using spades and hoes. Further land was bought so that 392⅖ acres (160

hectares) were owned by the university when it opened. Jefferson, as architect, was involved with design, layout and survey and as an official visitor with land purchase and financial control; he was in a sense both designer and client. He also organized the setting up of a brickyard on the west side where clay was dug, shaped in wooden moulds, naturally dried and then kiln-fired. He personally supervised production from time to time, which reached a peak of 180,000 bricks a month; not enough for all the work but probably a significant factor in the low cost of the buildings.

Also in 1817 on 6 October, only five months after Jefferson had written asking for comments on his preliminary proposals, the cornerstone was laid for the first pavilion in the presence of three presidents: Jefferson, James Madison and James Monroe. Pavilion VII is half way along the length of the west side of the site and differs from the subsequent pavilions by having an arcade of semi-circular arches on square piers on the ground floor. A single-storey portico is positioned above this.

During 1818 the State of Virginia considered setting up a university and three possible sites, of which the embryonic Central College in Charlottesville was one, were under consideration and debated at length. The commission, which was set up largely by Cabell, selected Charlottesville as the appropriate site and an act was passed on 25 January 1819. Jefferson had achieved his objectives.

The Lawn

A drawing done by Jefferson around 1820 – probably shaded by his granddaughter, Cornelia Jefferson Randolph – gives a bird's-eye view of the university campus, called the Lawn, from the east. It shows the layout in four rows and the individual pavilions Jefferson had been working on during the previous three years. The drawing is somewhat diagrammatic and does not show the Lawn stepping down from north to south nor the steep slope from the lawn to the eastern outer line of buildings. It also omits the serpentine walls that separated the rear gardens of the pavilions. The drawing fails to show the Rotunda at the head of the plan since it was not started until the other buildings were either complete or at least under construction. One of the great virtues of the design, as Jefferson had made clear, was that it could be built in stages as money became available.

The drawing shows two ranges, one on the east and the other on the west side of the academic village, also in brick but with discontinuous covered ways,

33

34

which contained student rooms and so-called hotels. These were refectories which were to feed between 25 and 50 students and were to be leased to hotel-keepers who would live there with their families. The kitchens, as in the pavilions, were in the basement. Jefferson more-over, wanted to lease the first hotel to a French family so that students might learn French at meal times. The hotels were visually desirable as punctuations of the outer ranges and as mirrors of the inner pavilions; a dispersal of eating places made for more flexible arrange-ments and prevented that centralization which Jefferson strove to avoid; addi-tionally, the particularity of each hotel might support an educational objective. The six hotels are thus typical of Jefferson's thinking.

The absence of the curving dividing walls on the aerial view also means that the 'necessaries', the privy outhouses, were not indicated. Jefferson had at first in his early plan for Pavilion VII shown these just to the rear of the pavilion, one for the professor and his family and one for students, entered separately. These were later wisely moved further out into the gardens and designed as

small brick buildings integral with the serpentine walls.

The garden walls that are such a char-acteristic feature of the university were not a Jeffersonian invention. They existed in England, most frequently in Suffolk, to provide shelter for plants and were also known to have been built on a plantation west of Jamestown around 1645. What is, however, characteristi-cally Jeffersonian is the calculation to demonstrate that serpentine walls are cheaper than walls with piers. Fewer bricks were needed and as bricklayers were paid by the number of bricks laid irrespective of alignment it could be demonstrated that the curved wall was more economical. It also coincided with a liking for curvilinear forms in garden design. The single brick construction meant, though, that the wall tended to be wet throughout its thickness and to be attacked by frost. All the walls have been rebuilt since 1949 on their original foun-dations during the reconstruction of the gardens but still need frequent attention.

The buildings of the university are in red brick laid mainly in Flemish bond so that stretchers and headers alternate. Windows, doors and shutters are painted softwood; some of the paint on the doors is grained to imitate mahogany, which could not be afforded. The roofs of the single-storey student rooms and colon-nade were covered by a series of ridges and valley gutters, which Jefferson called 'rooflets'. These were covered in tin and the rainwater drained to the rear. The appearance of a flat roof could thus be preserved. Unfortunately they leaked and were subsequently replaced by pitched slate roofs.

Each of the pavilions is different both in form and decoration. Most show their Palladian origins but two, Pavilion VIII, on the east side and Pavilion IX, on the west, reveal the hand of Latrobe and are clearly much more neo-classical in feel. Both have recessed entrance doors, which in the case of Pavilion VIII Jefferson labelled 'Latrobe's Lodge Front'. On his drawing of Pavilion IX he wrote down 'Latrobe' in the top right-hand corner.

The semi-circular recess of Pavilion IX is particularly successful, especially in its control of light. It undoubtedly owes something to the architecture of Ledoux, which Jefferson knew well. The semi-circular recess has a semidome, which is cut at its base by the continuous colon-nade; the opening therefore becomes a lunette, which allows light to strike the curved plaster surface of the niche. The shadows cast by the morning sun look like classic exercises in sciagraphy.

35

36

37

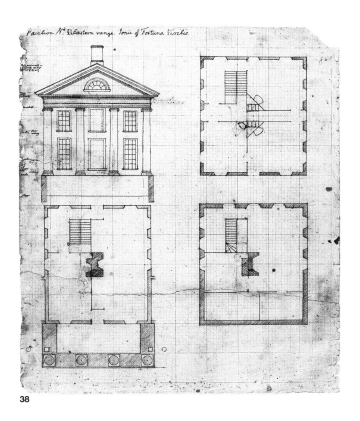

38

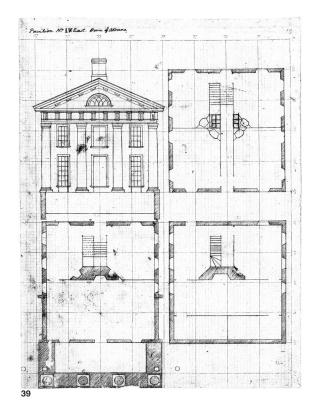

39

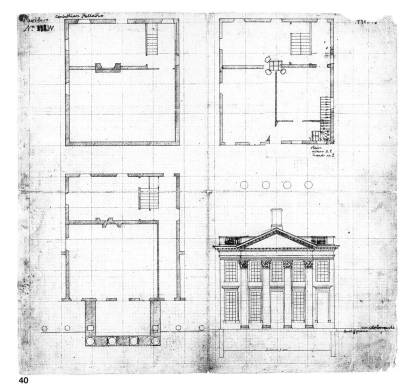

40

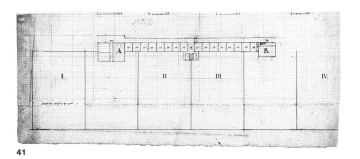

41

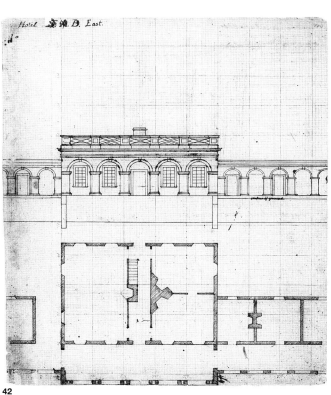

42

35 Steps leading to the beginning of the colonnade on the west side; the front door of Pavilion I is immeditely on the right.

36 Thomas Jefferson: the six-column portico of Pavilion V in the centre of the west side. This was the third pavilion to be erected. Jefferson's pre-1821 drawing shows a parapet with no pitched roof visible.

37 Thomas Jefferson: Pavilion VIII in the centre of the east side.

38 Thomas Jefferson: elevation and plans for Pavilion II, University of Virginia, 1819. The facade uses the Ionic order from the Temple of Fortuna Virilis in the Forum in Rome.

39 Thomas Jefferson: elevation and plans for Pavilion IV, University of Virginia, 1819. The Doric order from the Temple of Albano on the hills outside Rome is taken from a plate in Chambray's *Parallèle*; the words 'Doric of Albano' are in the top left-hand corner of Jefferson's drawing.

40 Thomas Jefferson: elevation and plans for Pavilion III, University of Virginia, 1818 or 1819. This was the second pavilion to be constructed. It uses a Corinthian order from Palladio.

41 Thomas Jefferson: plan of dormitories, West Range, with Hotels A and B, probably 1817. An early drawing before the final disposition of the outer line of buildings had been determined by Jefferson. The hotels were to include dining-rooms, kitchens in the basement, and quarters for housekeepers.

42 Thomas Jefferson: elevation and plan of Hotel D East, before 1822. The back of the drawing carries the note by Jefferson: 'Hotel with refectory and 2 family rooms with a flat roof and Chinese railing to be Tuscan also, but so much higher than the adjacent dormitories that it's entablature may be clear above theirs.'

43 Thomas Jefferson: elevation and plans for Pavilion VIII, University of Virginia, 1819. The design is based on the colossal order from the Baths of Diocletian. The recessed portico and facade may have been influenced by Latrobe; Jefferson referred to it as 'Latrobe's Lodge Front'.

44 Thomas Jefferson: elevation and plans for Pavilion IX, University of Virginia, before 1821. The most neo-classical pavilion inspired by the architecture of Claude-Nicolas Ledoux and perhaps also influenced by Latrobe, whose name Jefferson writes in the top right-hand corner.

45 Thomas Jefferson: study for garden walls, University of Virginia, c.1817–22. The calculation compares curved walls with a straight wall with 9-inch piers to show the economy of the curvilinear form.

46 Thomas Jefferson: elevation and section of University of Virginia dormitories, showing colonnades and 'rooflets'.

47, 48 Thomas Jefferson: section and elevation of the rotunda, University of Virginia, probably 1821. As in the Pantheon, the geometry of a sphere determines the dimensions; here roughly half those of the original.

49 Thomas Jefferson: plan of the first floor of the Rotunda, University of Virginia, probably 1821. The drawing shows a suite of three oval rooms reminiscent of the Désert de Retz Column House. The placement of the double staircase against the portico wall relates the landings to a view down the Lawn.

50 Thomas Jefferson: plan for the dome room of the Rotunda, University of Virginia, probably 1821. The library room under the dome was the single great indoor space of Jefferson's design; its position at the head of the Lawn is both architecturally and symbolically important.

51 Jean-Nicolas Le Rouge: Désert de Retz Column House, late 18th century.

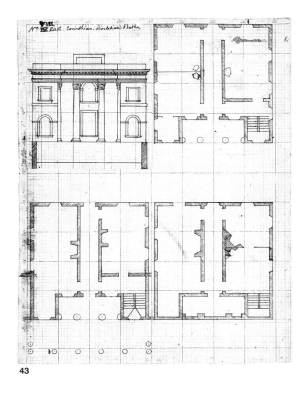

43

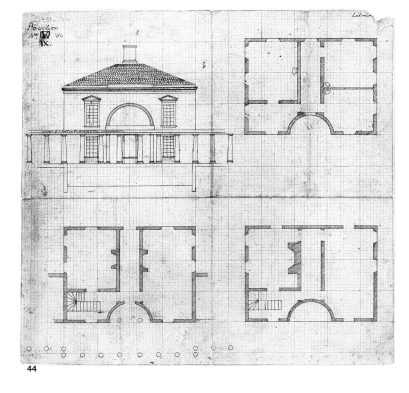

44

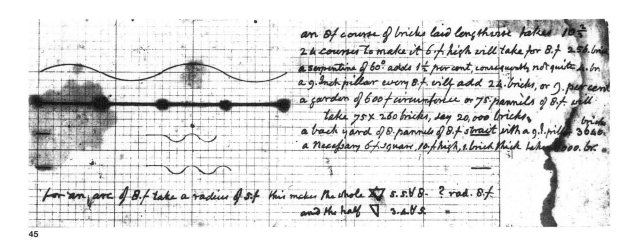

45

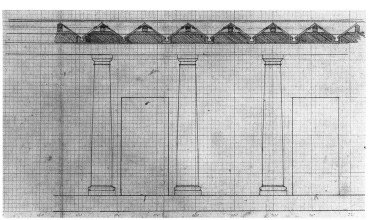

46

The Rotunda

The idea of the Rotunda is Latrobe's, the execution Jefferson's. The model was the Pantheon.

The drawings, which probably date from 1821, show a circle inscribed on section and elevation. The plan of the lower floors is a grouping of three oval rooms about a central space with a double curving staircase at the southern end and three tall windows that give a view down the lawn. Like Jefferson's suggestion for the Capitol in Washington, the plan is very close to the late 18th century Désert de Retz Column House, which he had described with great enthusiasm in a letter to Maria Cosway.

These oval rooms were to be used for lectures, examinations, religious worship, drawing, music or, as the Board of Visitors put in October 1824, 'any other of the innocent and ornamental accomplishments of life'.[15] The top floor under the dome was to be the library, the crowning room of the university. This dome room with an inner diameter of about 73 feet (22.25 metres), 77 feet externally, has the same proportions as the Pantheon but scaled down so that the diameter is half that of the original. As a result it dominates but does not overwhelm the north end of the Lawn and the pavilions on either side. The Rotunda is linked to the pavilions and the colonnade

by arcaded wings, which were to be used for gymnastic exercises by the students. The whole composition thus becomes a U-shaped enclosure facing south and open to the country at its lower end. The north side of the Rotunda was always considered by Jefferson as its back.

Notes exist that give Jefferson's calculations for the number of bricks needed for the Rotunda which he estimated to be 1,171,889. This was important in terms of procurement but was also a significant indication of cost. He drew a framing plan for the dome, and specified it as follows:

the thickness of the wall at the top, to wit, at the spring of the Vault of the roof is 22.i. on the top of the wall lay a curbed plate, in Delorme's manner, consisting of 4. thicknesses of 3.i. each. 22.i. wide, pieces 12.f. long, breaking joints every 3.f. bolted through with bolts of iron having a nut & screw at their end. on this curved plate the ribs of the roof are to rest. the ribs are to be 4. thicknesses of 1.i. plank in pieces 4.f. long, breaking joints at every foot. they are to be 18.i. wide, which leaves 4.i. of the plate for the Attic uprights to rest on.

the ribs are to be keyed together by cross boards at proper intervals from the ribs to head in as they shorten the curb of the sky light to be made also in Delorme's way, but vertically. the fireplaces and chimneys must be brought forward so that the flues may not make a hollow in the main walls.

they will thus become buttresses.[16]

Boullée had planned a cenotaph for Sir Isaac Newton in 1784 in which the interior of the sphere was a reproduction of the night sky. The stars were to be simulated by small shaft-like openings in the vault, which would let in daylight. Jefferson wanted something similar in paint: 'The Concave cieling of the Rotunda is proposed to be painted sky-blue and spangled with gilt stars in their position and magnitude copied exactly from any selected hemisphere of our latitude. a seat for the Operator movable and fixable at any point in the concave will be necessary, and means of giving every star it's exact position.'[17]

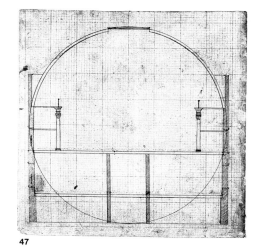

47

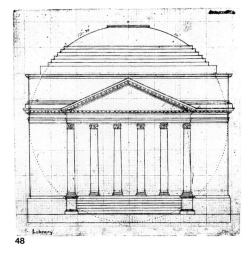

48

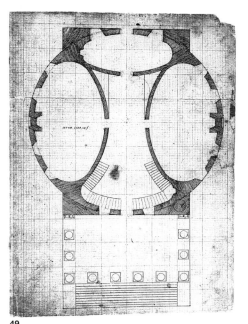

49

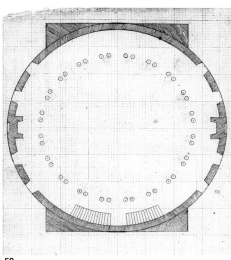

50

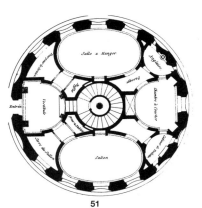

51

There then follows a sketch and extended description of the machinery for moving the operator. It is a kind of bo'sun's chair precariously suspended in space. There is no evidence that this suggestion was ever put into effect; perhaps the operation was more dangerous than Jefferson imagined.

Contracts were drawn up on 11 March 1823 and by August the brick walls were two-thirds of the way up to the underside of the roof. In October Corinthian capitals in marble were ordered from Italy and were shipped from Leghorn (Livorno). In May of the following year, square marble paving was also ordered from Italy. The suggestion was made that custom duties should not be charged since the capitals would be studied for educational purposes as 'superb models of antient Architecture'; like books they should be exempt.[18]

In June 1826 Jefferson, then in his eighty-third year, rode from Monticello to Charlottesville to see the Rotunda under construction. He sat in a chair at the head of the dome room stairs looking down the Lawn and watched the first of the Italian capitals being lifted into place. He stayed for about an hour and when the capital had been positioned, he went downstairs, mounted his horse and rode back to Monticello.[19]

Jefferson died on 4 July 1826, the fiftieth anniversary of the signing of the Declaration of Independence. He was buried the following day near his wife and youngest daughter in a private graveyard in the grounds of Monticello.

52

53

1826 to the present

The university formally opened on 7 March 1825 with sixty-eight students, so Jefferson had seen the fruition of his work. He had been the architect of the new institution in every sense of the word.

The library, though not the whole of the Rotunda, was finished in October 1826; the room had however been used earlier for a great ceremonial banquet on 5 November 1824 held in honour of the visit of the Marquis de Lafayette. Jefferson was said to have been so overcome by emotion that he could not respond to the toast in his honour.

In its early years the university was indeed a village surrounded by farm land. Plans from the middle of the 19th century show the fields nearby allocated to individual professors so that they could keep cows or grow produce. The earliest known photograph of the Lawn, taken in 1868, has in the foreground a large turnstile set in a wall on the south edge to keep out cattle and hogs. The university was designed with 108 rooms, each 12 feet 6 inches square (3.81 x 3.81 metres) intended for double occupancy. Enrolment was at first below capacity and tended to fluctuate; it was 123 in 1825, 177 in 1826, 128 in 1827, 131 in 1828 and 120 in 1829. In 1851 more teaching space was needed and an annexe was built to the north of the Rotunda. This was designed by Robert Mills who had received some architectural training from Jefferson. A portico was constructed on the north side and a portico was also inserted between the annexe and the Rotunda as a kind of open link. The columns had cast iron capitals modelled on the original marble Corinthian ones of the south portico. The building had considerable bulk but did not impinge on the Lawn; it did however give much more importance to the north side.

The North Annexe and Rotunda burnt down in a disastrous fire on the morning of 27 October 1895. Both buildings were gutted and only the charred round brick walls of the Rotunda were left standing. The annexe was never rebuilt; the Rotunda was dramatically changed inside during the reconstruction for which Stanford White was responsible. Judging by the photographs that exist, he created a noble high room for the library by losing the upper of the two

lower floors and incorporating it into the space beneath the dome. During 1973 to 1976 the building was returned on plan and section to its Jeffersonian original though a strong argument can be made for the fact that White's space was worth keeping as an architectural statement of its period. A whole system of ducts, electrical wiring and a lift was also secreted within the fabric during the most recent restoration.

Some changes to the buildings have been made externally but they are minimal. When seen in the brilliant sun against a blue sky the Rotunda represents more than any other building on the Lawn that neo-classical vision of a pure strong architecture deeply rooted in the mediterranean world of Athens and Rome. One is reminded of Karl Friedrich Schinkel's perspective of the front of the Palace of Orianda shimmering in the sun above a blue sea.

To replace the spaces lost in the north annexe, new buildings were planned at the lower, south end of the Lawn. White proposed a building on either side of the open end to preserve the view into the landscape. He was overruled by the Board of Visitors and a single building, Cabell Hall, now blocks that essential sense of continuity to an outside space.

Originally several of the pavilions – III, V, VIII and X – had balustrades and parapets, which gave them a cubic appearance. Equally in the single-storey link-blocks the so-called rooflets meant that the Chinese balustrades were dominant and the impression that the roofs were an upper terrace was much more marked. Since the replacement of the rooflets the pavilions have looked somewhat more Palladian and less neo-classical than at first conceived.

None of these alterations and additions however have marred the general impression of Jefferson's conception. It remains the noblest spatial relation of buildings and landscape, quintessentially American and the finest suburban (in the very best sense of the word) architectural composition in the United States, perhaps anywhere in the world.

52 Karl Friedrich Schinkel: project for a Palace at Orianda, 1838. This perspective shows a palace on the Crimean coast poised on a rock above the sea; an ideal classical world-re-created in the 19th century.

53 The south-facing portico of the Rotunda seen from the terrace above the arcaded podium; the space below the terraces was used by students for gymnastics and games.

54 Thomas Jefferson: plan of roof framing for the Rotunda, University of Virginia, before April 1821. The specification describes the size and placement of the timber members.

55 Thomas Jefferson: 'Machinery for moving the Operator'. Jefferson hoped to paint the underside of the dome in the Rotunda blue and to depict the night sky; the sketch and description explain a means of suspending a painter in space and of locating the stars on the hemisphere.

54

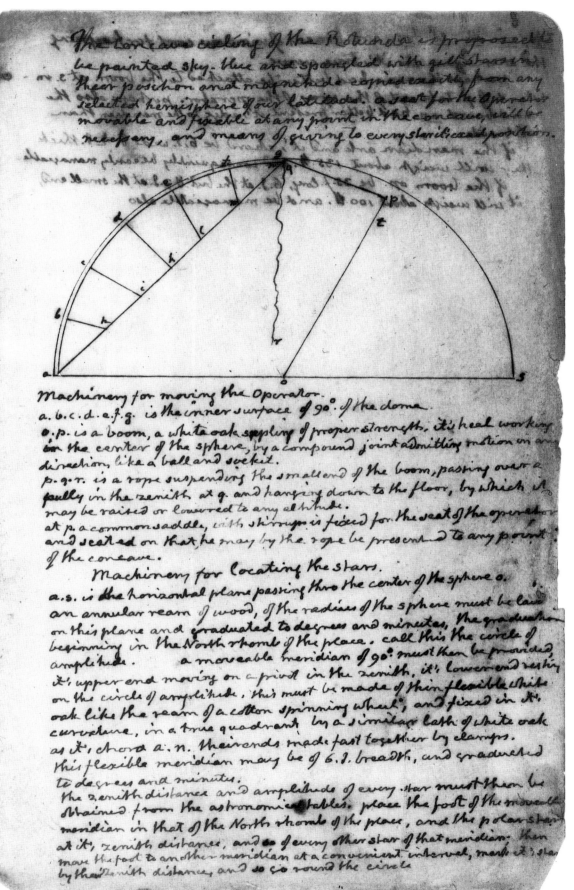

55

57

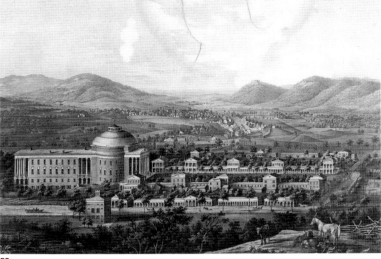

58

59

56 William A. Pratt: plan of University Cleared Land, drawn between 1856 and 1869. The plan of the area surrounding the university marks the allocation of fields to particular professors.

57 Earliest-known photograph of the Lawn, 1868. This photograph, taken from the south, shows the wall, gates and turnstile that existed to keep out livestock.

58 View of the University of Virginia, Charlottesville and Monticello, from Lewis Mountain, 1856. A lithograph 'drawn from nature and printed in colours' by F. Sachse & Co and published by C. Bohn, Washington & Richmond. The north addition to the Rotunda and the Rotunda itself are rather too large; the way the 'academical village' is surrounded by farming land however is very obvious.

59 University of Virginia, from the south, 1856. An engraving also produced by C. Bohn; the Anatomical Theatre with its pyramidal roof is visible on the right.

60 Clarence Stein and Henry Wright: plan for Radburn, New Jersey, 1927. This plan segregates people from cars by creating U-shaped building groups whose pedestrian side opens on to a communal lawn.

61 Thomas Jefferson: elevations, plans and section of the Anatomical Theatre, University of Virginia, 1825. This is the last building Jefferson designed and it was not completed until after his death. The ground floor was labelled 'Museum?' and the roof with a central skylight uses Jefferson's favourite device of tinplate covered 'ridge-and-furrow' roofs; the neo-classical cubicular form is thus preserved.

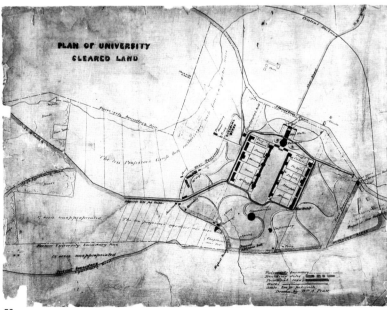

56

The inheritance

Jefferson was born 250 years ago. His political thought and example continue to exert an influence, even though he would be astonished by the changes that have occurred in American society. This would be especially true of its urbanization. Significantly, William Jefferson Clinton inaugurated his presidency as well as the celebrations of Jefferson's anniversary by starting his journey to Washington in Charlottesville.

The influence of Jefferson's architecture and of the University of Virginia in particular has also been evident in a number of ways. These in no way depend on Jefferson's achievements as a politician and thinker though both are clearly the work of a single remarkable personality. The buildings, gardens and 520 surviving drawings stand in their own right.

A general Jeffersonian influence can be discerned in the work of Frederick Law Olmstead – designer of Central Park, New York, Riverside Chicago and university sites, and campaigner for the preservation of Niagra Falls and Yosemite Valley – and through him those who followed in the American environmental tradition. Many of the views of Lewis Mumford, for instance, are close to those of Jefferson. The most direct influence probably occurs in the work of Clarence Stein. The attempts he and Henry Wright made at Radburn, New Jersey in 1927 to lay out suburban super blocks with car-free central greens have been copied frequently elsewhere. The plan is a series of U-shaped green areas, which at their open end link the larger linear green spaces; service roads penetrate into the gaps to make car 'closes'. It is the plan of the university multiplied.

I first saw Jefferson's university in the spring of 1955 while visiting the dams and other works of the Tennessee Valley Authority that had been instigated by Franklin D. Roosevelt. Like the university these were attempts by another president to help the less developed South and to shift the centre gravity from the East Coast.

Apart from the great visual pleasure of the Lawn – green, red brick, white paint – two ideas became apparent to me and left a strong impression. The first is how Jefferson's composition provides for diversity within unity. Each pavilion, like each person, is unique, yet the social grouping has a unity that marks it as an entity, as a university, within nature. Jefferson certainly saw the emergent democratic society of the United States in that way. His first thoughts about the layout with only pavilions and no hierarchically important Rotunda at the centre was probably nearer the political analogue but architecturally weaker. Jefferson was always against a strong centre in government. To paraphrase a sentence in his 'Notes on Virginia', he 'aimed to devise a government too weak to aid the wolves and yet strong enough to protect the sheep'.[20]

That unity in diversity, moreover, had a nobility that made for an architecture that in turn celebrated every user. To this day it is a coveted honour among students at the university to win a room on the Lawn. Every visitor must also feel some sense of ennoblement.

The second idea, which on reflection becomes important is that the form, the permanent organization of the university is created by residential buildings. In this it is very close to Oxford and Cambridge. A few years after my first visit I was involved in the planning of one of the new British universities and also started to write about university planning in general. What became obvious was that university buildings could be categorized by their degree of permanence; laboratories were the least permanent, student residences and small seminar rooms the most permanent. It seemed sensible therefore that the armature of a university should be created by its most permanent buildings. This is precisely what Jefferson had done at Charlottesville. Interestingly the only building that he designed outside the area of the Lawn, an Anatomical Theatre, which dates from the year before his death, was demolished in 1938 to allow the building of a large new library.

In the minds of some the Jeffersonian architectural legacy lies in its demonstration that buildings based on classical forms and proportions have a validity for all periods. Although Jefferson acted on that proposition, I do not believe that it represents his desires. He had no taste for either absolutes or a continuous reference to the past. On the contrary he found Aristotle and other classical authors, for example, of little relevance; 'so different was the style of society then, and with those people, from what is now with us, that I think little edification can be obtained from their writings on the subject of government'.[21]

In architecture he also hoped for an indigenous growth that would run parallel with the development of the new republic. At a quite small, detailed level, Jefferson encouraged Latrobe to create an 'American Order' and Latrobe sent him letters with drawings of capitals based on corn, cotton and tobacco plants to be installed in the Capitol building.

The essential need of the newly independent States was for orderly growth and the transformation of a largely untamed land. Building was a key element. The Jeffersonian circle understood this and thus strongly conceived the Creator as an architect and builder. To be President and Architect was therefore in no way an incongruous combination, for the greatest compliment which could be paid any man was that his mind mirrored God's works. Every architect's and builder's thoughts must be directed towards the future for which the work is, after all, intended. Or as Jefferson once put it: 'I like the dreams of the future better than the history of the past'.

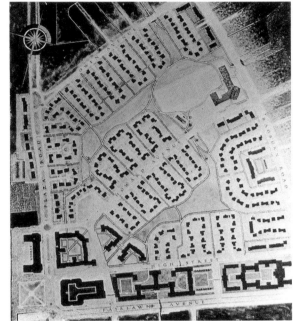

60

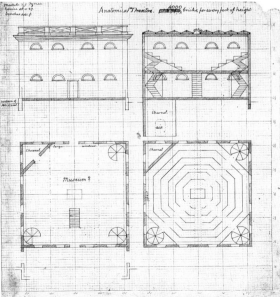

61

24

Acknowledgements

The author is very grateful to Professor Robert L. Vickery Jr who made it possible for him to stay in Pavilion VII and thus to experience the Lawn fully; John G. Waite of Mesick · Cohen · Waite · Architects in Albany, New York, who very generously made available their survey drawings for this publication; Dr James Murray Howard, Architect for the Historic Buildings and Grounds, University of Virginia, and his staff who drew his attention to various sources; to the Curator of Manuscripts and staff of the University Archives of the University of Virginia Library and the Librarian and staff of the Massachusetts Historical Society, Boston, who allowed him to study Jefferson's original drawings and gave permission for their reproduction; Richard Cheek who enthusiastically involved himself in photographing the Lawn; John Hewitt for preparing the main drawings for publication.

Essay illustrations were provided by the Bridgeman Art Library (25), Collection of the Library of Congress (29), Coolidge Collection, Massachusetts Historical Society (2, 7–9, 11, 12, 15–17, 19), Manuscript Print Collection, Special Collections Department, University of Virginia Library (56–59), New York State Historical Association (1), Photothèque des Musées de la Ville de Paris (4), Robert Lautman (14), Thomas Jefferson Papers, Special Collections Department, Manuscripts Division, University of Virginia Library (10, 18, 28, 30, 24, 38–50, 62–5).

Notes

The spelling and punctuation in the quotations are as in the original; Jefferson's usage is not necessarily consistent, nor does it always correspond to present-day practice.

1 Manuscript in Massachusetts Historical Society, Boston.
2 Nichols, 1976, p.164.
3 Boorstin, 1981, p.8.
4 Nichols, 1976, p.168.
5 Scully, 1991, p.336.
6 Nichols and Griswold, 1986, p.139.
7 Nichols and Griswold, 1986, p.41.
8 Nichols and Griswold, 1986, p.46.
9 Nichols and Griswold, 1986, p.153.
10 Nichols and Griswold, 1986, p.148.
11 Adams, 1992, p.286.
12 O'Neal, 1960, p.19.
13 Palladio, 1965, p.48.
14 Boorstin, 1981, p.217.
15 Adams, 1992, p.295.
16 O'Neal, 1960, p.52, document 93.
17 O'Neal, 1960, p.52, document 94.
18 O'Neal, 1960, p.40, document 66.
19 Hogan, 1987, p.26.
20 Boorstin, 1981, p.190.
21 Boorstin, 1981, p.212.
22 Mesick · Cohen · Waite · Architects, 1991, p.33.

Bibliography

Adams, William Howard *Jefferson's Monticello*, New York, 1983.
Adams, William Howard (ed.) *The Eye of Thomas Jefferson*, Charlottesville and Columbia, (1976) 1992.
Boorstin, Daniel J. *The Lost World of Thomas Jefferson*, Chicago, (1948) 1981.
Guinness, Desmond and Sadler Jr, Julius Trousdale *Mr Jefferson, Architect*, New York, 1973.
Hogan, Pendleton *The Lawn: a Guide to Jefferson's University*, Charlottesville, 1987.
Kimball, Fiske *Thomas Jefferson: Architect* (with a new introduction by Frederick D. Nichols) New York, 1968. (facsimile edition of first publication in 1916)
McLaughlin, Jack *Jefferson & Monticello: the Biography of a Builder*, New York, 1988.
Mesick · Cohen · Waite · Architects 'Pavilion VI University of Virginia Historic Structure Report' Albany, NY, 1991
Nichols, Frederick Doveton 'Jefferson: the Making of an Architect' in *Jefferson & the Arts: an Extended View* (ed. William Howard Adams) Washington, 1976.
Nichols, Frederick Doveton *Thomas Jefferson's Architectural Drawings*, Charlottesville (1960), 1978.
Nichols, Frederick Doveton and Griswold, Ralph E. *Thomas Jefferson, landscape architect*, Charlottesville (1978), 1986.
Norton, Paul F. 'Thomas Jefferson & the Planning of the National Capital' in *Jefferson & the Arts: an Extended View* (ed. William Howard Adams) Washington, 1976.

O'Neal, William B. *Jefferson's Buildings at the University of Virginia; the Rotunda*, Charlottesville, 1960.
O'Neal, William B. *Pictorial History of the University of Virginia*, Charlottesville, 1976.
Palladio, Andrea *The Four Books of Architecture* (Isaac Ware translation, 1738), New York, 1965.
Scully, Vincent *Architecture: the natural & man-made*, New York, 1991.
Tavernor, Robert *Palladio and Palladianism*, London, 1991.

The twenty-volume 'definitive' edition of Jefferson's writings is *The Writings of Thomas Jefferson* (ed. Albert Ellery Bergh) Washington DC, 1907.

Chronology

6 May 1810
Detailed description of a proposal for a new university by Jefferson presented in a letter to the Trustees of East Tennessee College
circa 1815
Early site plan prepared for a new university by Jefferson
5 May 1817
Site approved by Board of Visitors
9 May 1817
Jefferson sends sketch layout to Dr Thornton and on 12 May 1817 to Benjamin Latrobe
18 July 1817
Jefferson surveys site, aged seventy-four
24 July 1817
Latrobe sends sketch of layout with Rotunda to Jefferson
6 October 1817
Cornerstone laid for Pavilion VII in the presence of three presidents: Thomas Jefferson, James Madison and James Monroe
25 January 1819
Act Establishing University passed by State Legislature
30 September 1821
Pavilions III, V, VII and IX completed
circa 1821
Drawings prepared for Rotunda
7 October 1822
Construction starts on Rotunda
7 March 1825
University formally opened
June 1826
Jefferson pays last visit to university
4 July 1826
Jefferson dies in his eighty-third year
October 1826
Rotunda completed
27 October 1895
Fire destroys most of Rotunda

Photographs

26 **Previous page** The Rotunda and Pavilion II seen from the balcony of Pavilion I. The terraces on both sides of the Rotunda, the balconies of the pavilions and roofs of the dormitories provide a controlling horizontal line above which the more important buildings rise.

Left Pavilion IX terminates the west side. Its entrance is recessed in a semi-circular niche with a semi-dome open above the line of the balcony to let in light. It is the most neo-classical of all the pavilions and owes a good deal to Ledoux and probably to Latrobe. It could be argued that Jefferson placed the most classical pavilions near the Rotunda and the most clearly neo-classical ones at the open, southern end.

Right The entrance to Pavilion IX is a white, plastered, semi-circular recess. The two leaves of the central door are painted green and are curved like the wall.

Pavilion VII, in the middle of the   29
west side, was designed in 1817
and was the first to be built. It is the
only pavilion that has an arcaded
front as the continuation of
the covered way. Jefferson may
have intended at first that all the
pavilions should have this form.

Left Pavilion I on the west side is based on the Doric order taken from Diocletian's Baths in Rome, Pavilion II on the opposite side of the Lawn uses the Ionic order, the Rotunda between them is Corinthian; the major orders of classical architecture are thus visible next to each other; an intended lesson in architectural history. The balcony, which is a visual continuation of the roofs of the dormitories, is hung by iron rods from the roof.

Right The Doric columns of Pavilion I are white-painted plaster. The bases and capitals are concrete and were made in Charlottesville.

Following page The Lawn from the south; the even-numbered pavilions are on the east side, the odd-numbered on the west. Each of the ten pavilions was intended for a professor teaching in one of the ten schools.

Left The original Corinthian marble capitals of the Rotunda were badly damaged in the fire of 1895 and had to be replaced.

Right The south front of the Rotunda and the steps leading down to the Lawn; construction started in October 1822 and finished in September 1826, two months after Jefferson's death. The entire building was badly damaged in the fire of 27 October 1895 and was then largely rebuilt.

Left and right The Jeffersonian university consisted of four parallel rows running north–south; the two inner rows were the ten pavilions and linking student rooms, the two outer rows consisted of hotels and again lines of student rooms, in this instance, behind an arcaded walk-way. The hotels were the student refectories. Their architecture is simpler than that of the pavilions and they could be considered the farm ranges of the 'academical village'.

Centre The gardens of the pavil-ions are divided by serpentine walls one brick thick. Linked to these walls and some distance from the house are small brick garden pavil-ions, which are the 'necessaries' or privvies. At intervals, alleys go through to the colonnade and pro-vide service access to the pavilions and especially to the kitchens in the basement.

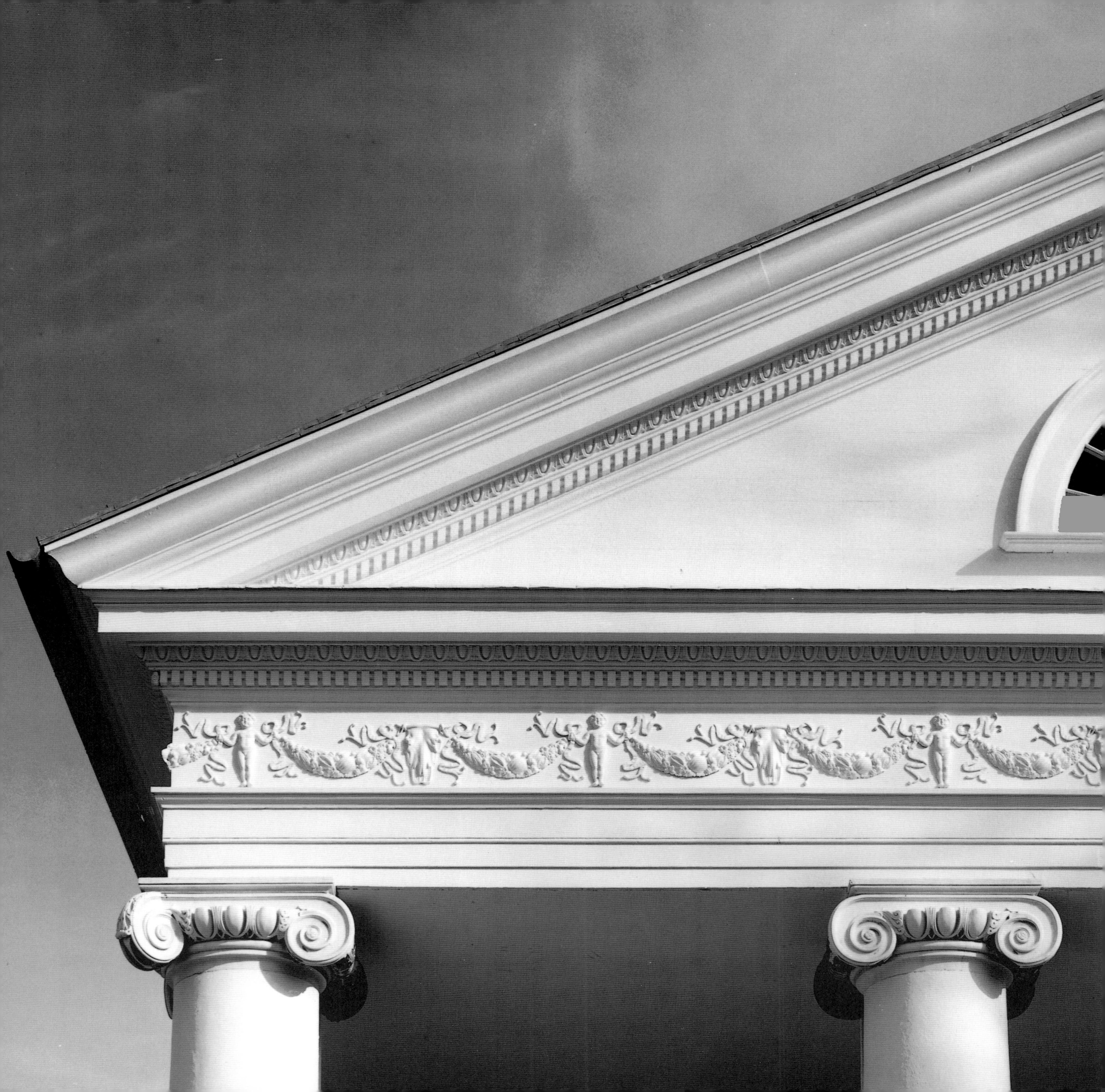

Left The Ionic capitals of Pavilion II were in the first shipment of Carrara marble capitals received from Italy. The columns are plastered brick. The frieze consists of ox skulls and cherubs linked by a garland, a motif which Jefferson was to use later in the cornice of the north oval room in the Rotunda.

Right Pavilion II on the east side is directly opposite Pavilion I; the Rotunda on its podium is between them. The lunette in the tympanum and the windows below the terrace at the side of the Rotunda follow the same pattern. The balcony is separated from the columns by a gap of about 100 mm and is hung from the pedimented roof by four iron rods.

Left Pavilion VI; the lawn slopes down on the right.
Right The front door of Pavilion I. The doors are grained with a reddish brown paint to simulate mahogany, which was too expensive to use. The trim was an off-white colour.

42 **Left** Pavilion X at the southern end of the east side; there is a single student room on on the right. The original elevation was much more neo-classical since Jefferson intended the pediment to be surmounted by a dominant parapet.
Right Pavilion X, like Pavilion IX on the other side, has a single student room attached, which can be interpreted as the end of the colonnade or as the beginning of an extension of the university; it is very likely that Jefferson did not think of his plan as finite.

44 The line of student rooms is interrupted occasionally by openings that link the rear service alleys to the colonnade. The pavilions of the west side can be seen across the stepped lawn.

Pavilion VI

(pavilions I–X and hotels A–F are shown, right). The decision to build this pavilion, located at the centre of the east side of the Lawn, was taken in the summer of 1819. Serious construction work did not seem to start until 1821.

Jefferson prepared drawings on his usual graph paper, notes and specifications. These gave dimensions and at the top of the page also had the words 'Ionic of the theatre of Marcellus'. Presumably Jefferson based the design of the orders on plates of the Theatre of Marcellus in Rome, possibly those in Roland Fréart de Chambray's *Parallèle de l'Architecture Antique avec la Moderne*, of 1766.

Separate contractors were employed for brickwork, masonry, plastering, painting, glazing and the tin plate covering the roof. Jefferson wrote enthusiastically about the merits of the tin plate, which was imported from Britain: 'I would advise you to cover with tin rather than shingles. It is the lightest and most durable cover in the world. We know it will last 100 years, and how much more we do not know'.[22]

At the end of 1824 the total cost of construction was recorded as $9,737.42.

The first professor to inhabit the pavilion was Thomas Hewitt Key, who was employed to teach mathematics, navigation, architecture and astronomy.

The first addition to the building was made around 1831 and consisted of extending the basement at the rear, probably for more servant accommodation.

A porch was later added on top. Subsequent additions occurred between 1860 and 1875. Central steam heating was installed during 1899–1900 and the first electric light bill is for 1900–1. Extensive renovation was carried out during 1954 under the supervision of Frederick D. Nichols, an authority on Jefferson's architecture.

The drawings of Pavilon VI are survey drawings of the building as it existed in 1990. They form part of an extensive historic structure report by Mesick · Cohen · Waite · Architects submitted to the Jeffersonian Restoration Advisory Board in 1991.

46

Site plan

This is based on a plan of the Jeffersonian university drawn by John Neilson, engraved by Peter Maverick and published in 1822. The original plan was later used in a prospectus for the university.

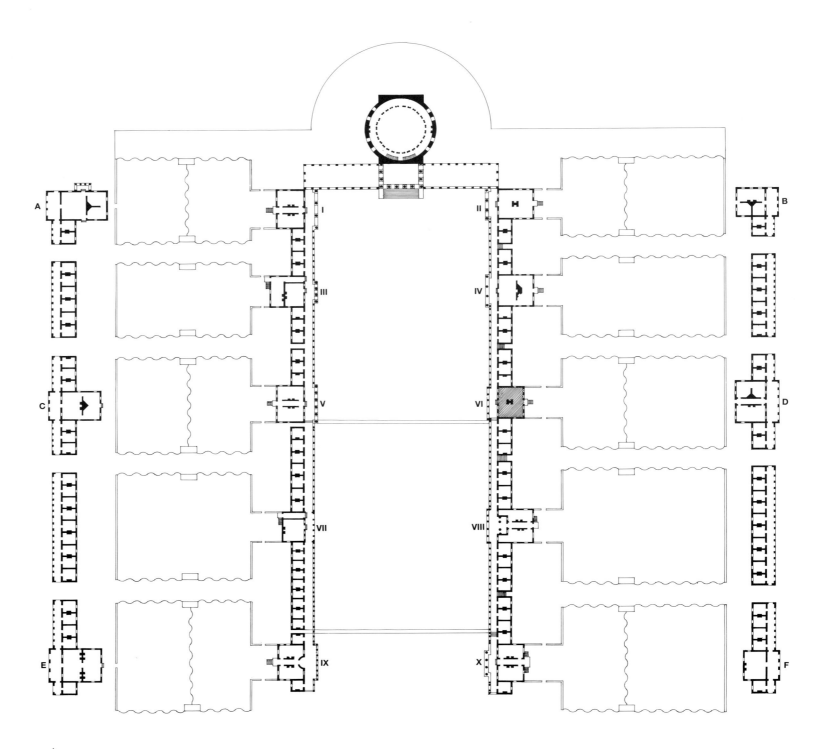

0   20m

0   60ft

Isometric site plan
This aerial view of the Lawn from the south-east shows the gardens as planted by the Garden Club of Virginia between 1948 and 1965. There were no designs for the gardens by Jefferson; the present layout is by Alden Hopkins. Pavilion VI is shown in the following pages.

Drawings

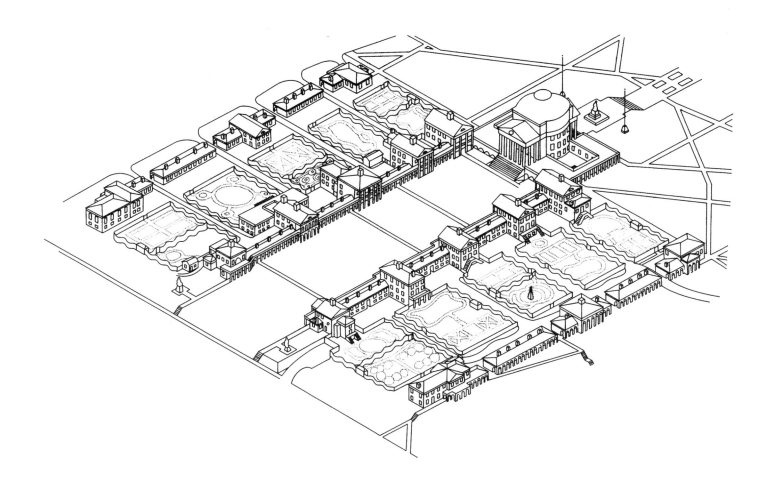

Floor plans

Basement

1 stair hall
2 north-west room,
   originally kitchen
3 pipe room, part of former kitchen
4 laundry room, original
   use not known
5 bedroom
6 hall
7 bathroom, created in 1954

Ground floor

1 entrance hall
2 study, originally part of
   professor's living quarters
3 stair hall
4 rear hall, altered in 1954
   renovation
5 living room, original lecture room
6 pantry, part of 1954 renovation
7 lavatory, part of 1954 renovation
8 kitchen, part of 1954 renovation
9 dining-room, part of late
   19th-century addition

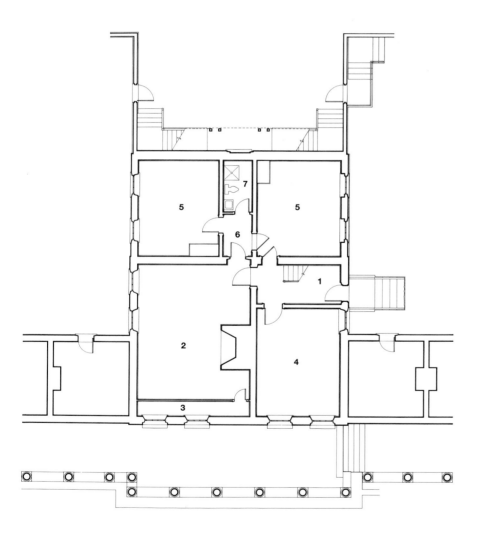

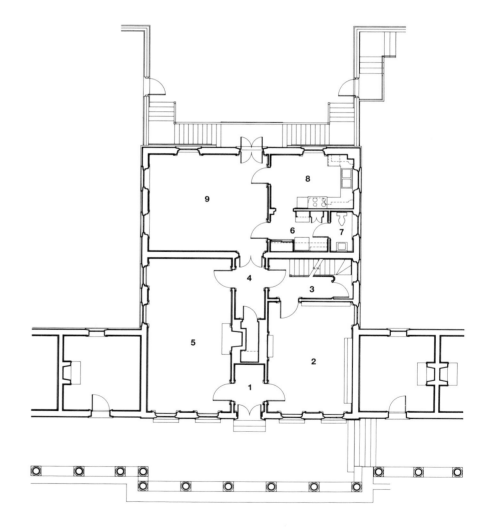

0   3m

0   10ft

First floor

1 stair hall
2 bedroom
3 hall
4 bedroom, originally the
   professor's parlour
5 rear hall, part of 1954 renovation
6 closet
7 bathroom, part of
   1954 renovation
8 dressing room, part of
   1954 renovation
9 bedroom, remodelled in 1928

Attic

1 storage, original brick wall on
   east side removed during late
   19th-century addition and rebuilt
   at east end

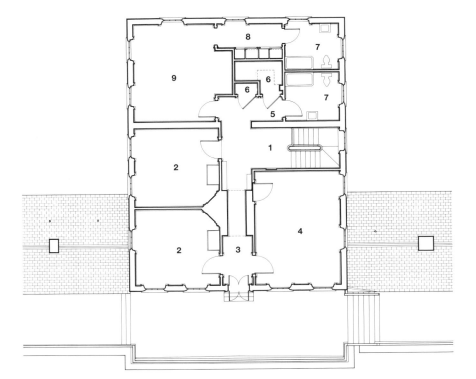

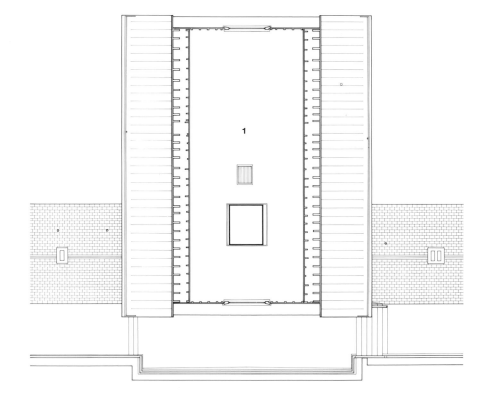

50

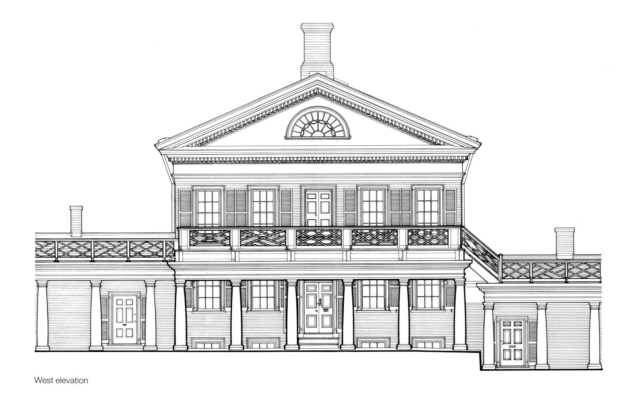

West elevation

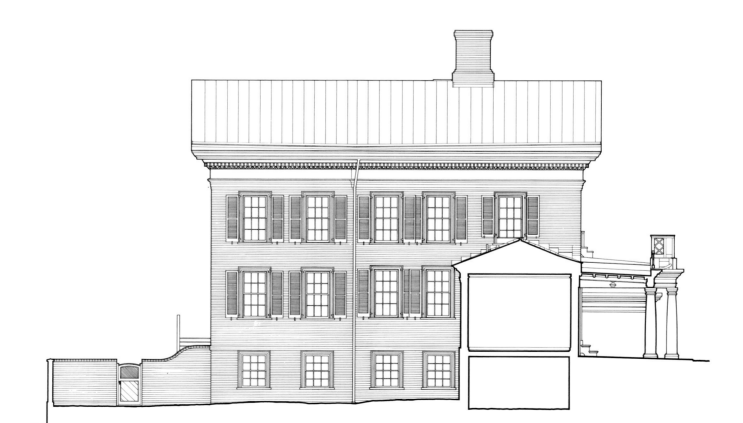

North elevation

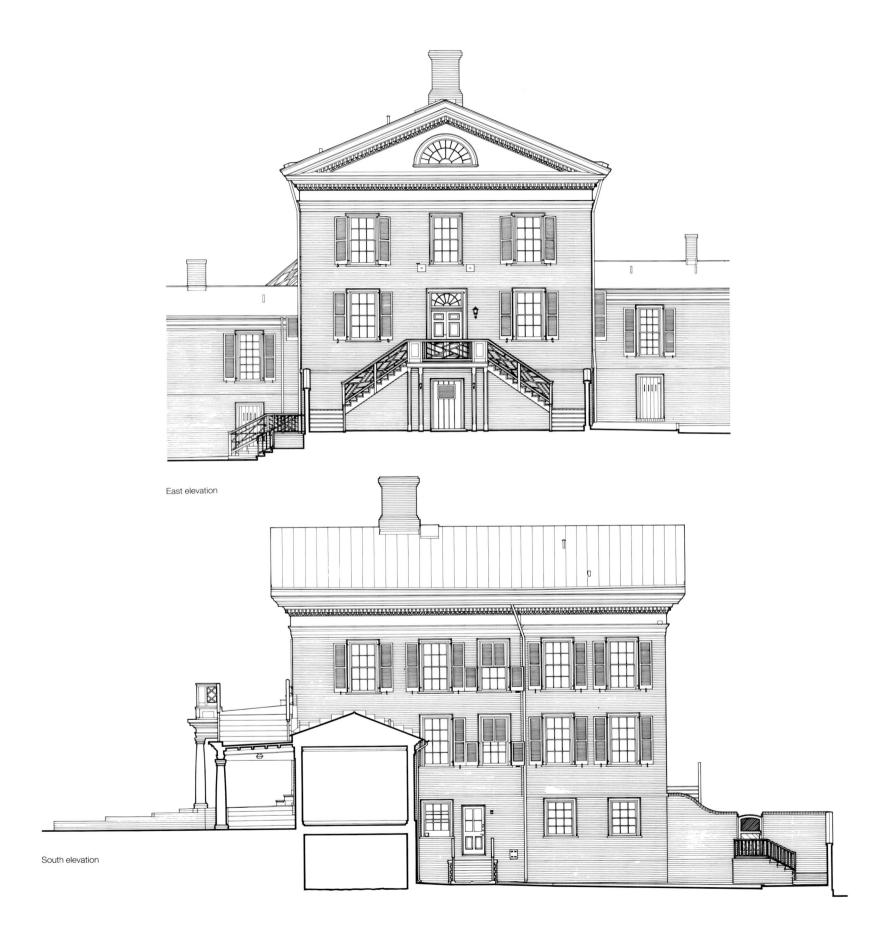

East elevation

South elevation

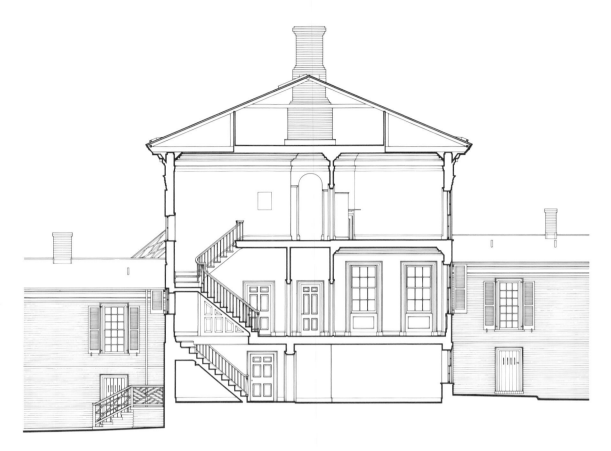

Cross section looking west through stairway

Cross section looking west

Longitudinal section looking south

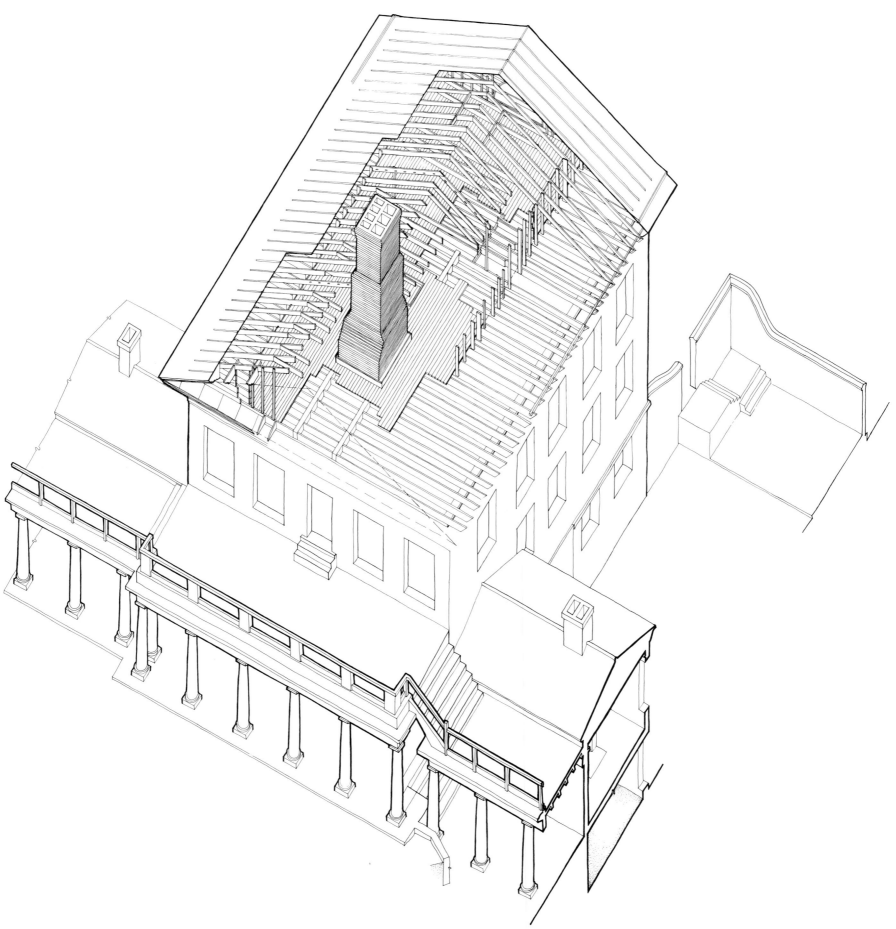

Attic floor detail

Joists are connected with
a pegged mortice and tenon to
a plate bearing on a masonry wall.

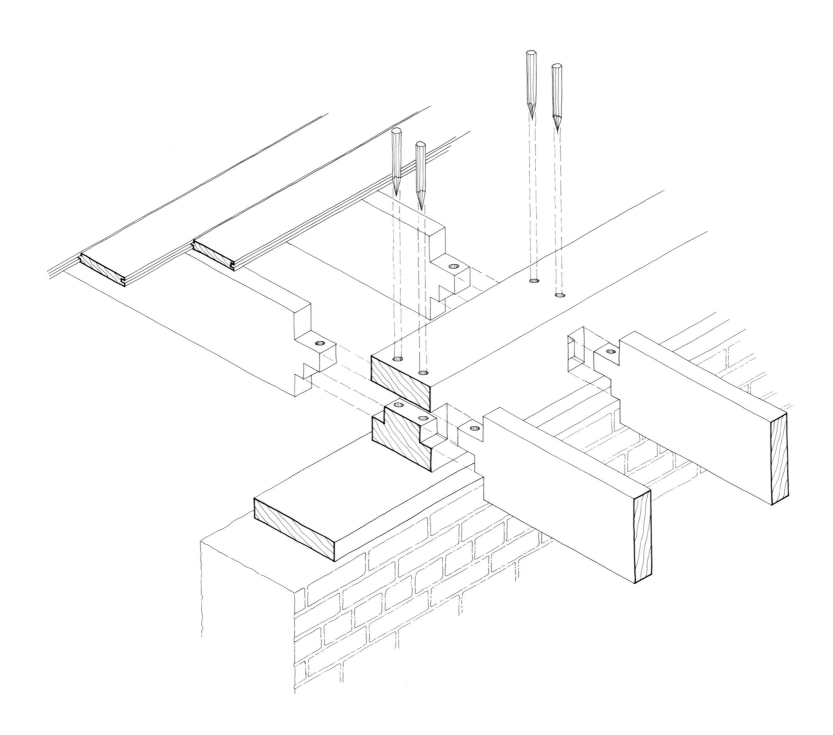

Mantel elevations and details
Left, ground floor study (room
two); right, ground floor living-
room (room five). Both mantels are
reproductions installed in 1954.

0   50mm

0   2in

Study

Living room

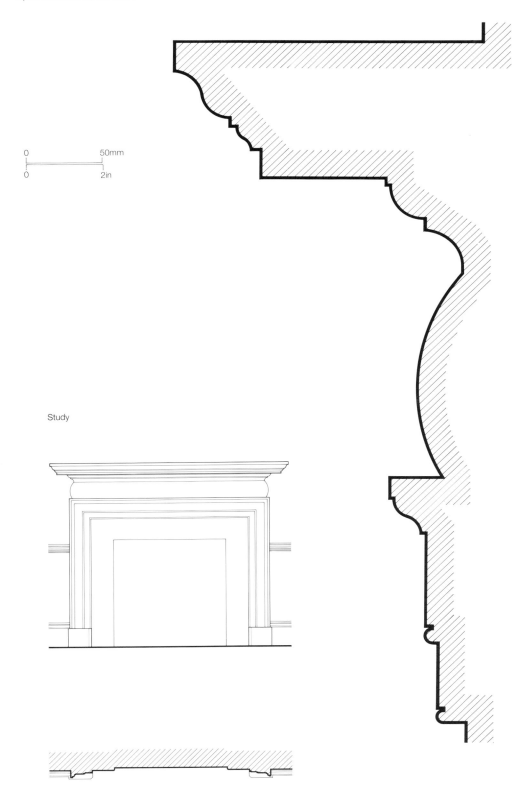

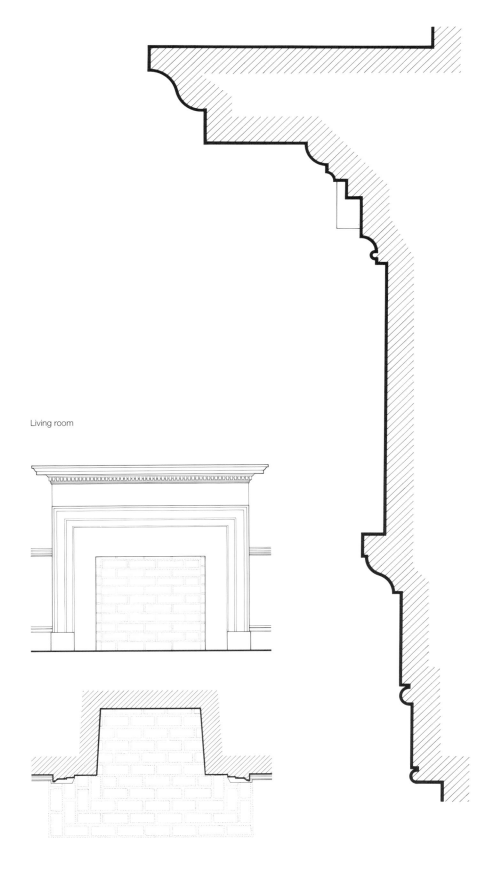

0   500mm

0   18in

Moulding profiles
Top, chair rail profiles; centre and
bottom, baseboard profiles.

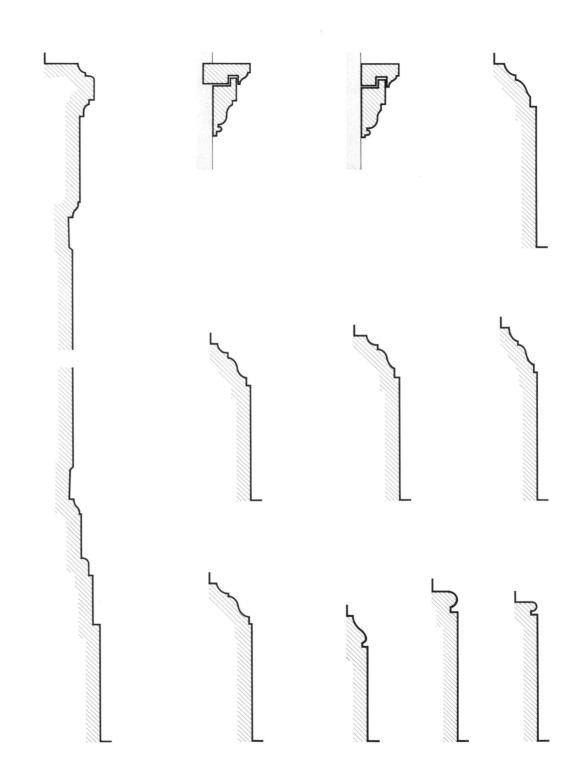

0   100mm

0   4in

Cornice and entablature
An original detail in a professor's living-room (room four on the first floor, shown far right). The terracotta heads and cast-lead ribbons were provided by William Coffee who frequently worked with Jefferson.

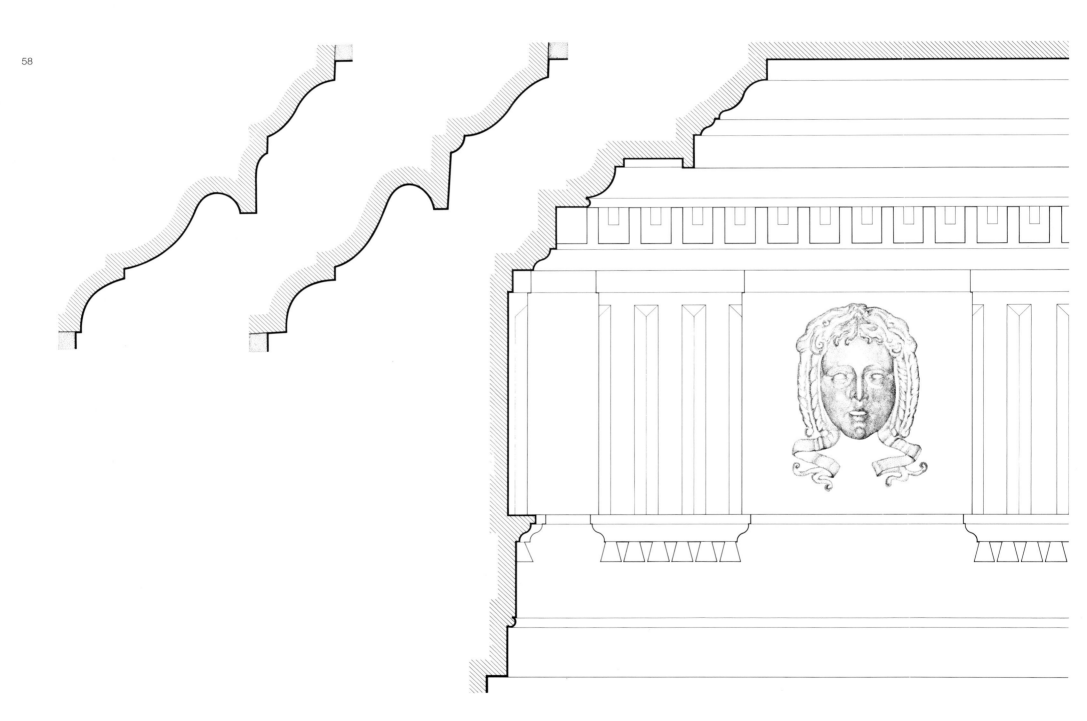

0   100mm

0   4in

Window trim profiles

Door trim profiles

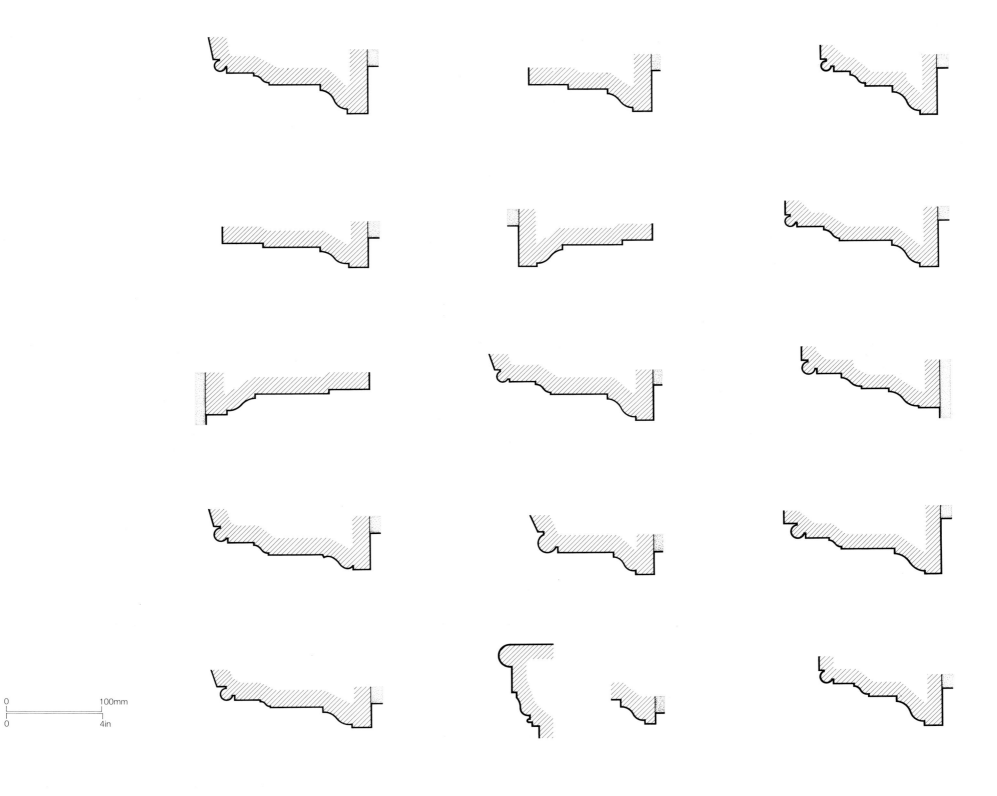

0 ⊢————————⊣ 100mm
0   4in

0   1m

0   3ft

0   100mm

0   4in